A Lady of Letters

Fareh Iqbal

Copyright © 2017 Fareh Iqbal
All rights reserved.
Bella Books
ISBN 13: 978-1775076124
ISBN-10: 1775076121

*The journey does not end
merely because the heart breaks.*

Please

do not request

lines of symmetry

of lovers' beauty

and Shakespearean sonnets

dedicated to a gentle love,

for the poet knows only

the crumbling ruins

of heartbreak

that would rival

the downfall

of an empire.

The architecture

of a well-crafted sentence

possesses the strength

to break human hearts

and move

the most stubborn

of mountains.

Are poems not love letters

from a writer

seducing their readers

with words

beckoning them

to delve a little deeper

and become one

with the ink.

Where can one seek solace

when their own skin

fits like a stranger.

We are

wrapped

in cocoons of discomfort

bound

in suits of flesh

we no longer recognize

resigned

to life as caterpillars

when we were born

to be butterflies.

Muse

Her enchantment
wove a spell
so effortless and true
humbling himself before her
he declared
she was not the poet
but the muse.

Her touch

danced upon

the surface of his skin

as his words

broke into waves

that coursed through her veins,

it was a moment

precious to her memory

slipping through the syllables

of her inadequate poetry

yearning to capture the

beating heart of a second.

She manifested herself
in the tales she wove
characters and lifetimes
sharing the same soul
bound as one
in a fictional kaleidoscope.

Are the poets doomed

to recall the beauty

of what may have been,

living in a daze

of the glory

that never quite happened

forever doubting

the taste of their memories?

The perfume of pen and paper

is an elixir for the poet

a fragrance that captures

human plight and dystopian adventure,

a pilgrim's journey

marching bravely

into the hearts

of their beloved readers.

Bloodlust and revenge

do not to the writer appeal

for her pen is mightier

than their swords

and the written word

possesses the celestial power

to protect and heal.

She captured his soul

and poured it

into the ink

that stained her paper

hues of grey

and shades of pink.

The scratch of

ink on paper

was a melody

to her ears

that rejoiced in

its temporary remedy.

Her turbulent heart

was caught between

struggle

and surrender

a torment that did not soften

with the passing of the seasons.

Her sense of time

dissolved like a dying star

lost in the sky's glittering canopy

where the doubts of youth

were alien planets

that revolved around

a distant galaxy.

The afternoon passed

in a haze

of three cups of tea

that stained her lips

Moroccan pink

entwined with

the careful deduction

of theology

that saturated her mind

with colours

most succinct.

His lips

spun a song

on her skin

that would take

a decade

to fade.

Her hope floats

along the Norwegian sea

kissing the water

from which he drinks

turning the tide

from empty blue

to ripples

of cerise pink.

Awoken

by the cry of a lark

her eyes sought his form

caressing his features

like a beloved heirloom

as the dawn broke free

bleeding crimson and gold

into the cavity of her room.

Entwined
until the salt
of your skin
melts
with mine.

Her thoughts
were drenched
in honey,
heavy
with golden luster,
feeding off
the reminisces
of their queen.

The perfect reflection
of what dwells
in the heavens
lies upon the face
of thy beloved.

He was

as familiar to her

as her own reflection

every nuance

of his flesh

a beautiful

remembrance.

The dappled sunlight
rippled across her skin
like waves of caramel
reaching for
his familiar golden shore.

She slipped

through his fingertips

and perished

on a sigh

restless

for the salvation

of his touch.

In a pair of worn brown shoes
his curious feet
brought him to her
in a haven of books
he offered her a lifeline
on the string of a kite
to the skies and wonder.

Her words

perished

on a breath

through rusted lips

that could not part

to lend syllables

a voice

and thoughts

a heart.

Philadelphia

Take me where
the sun always shines
back to the summer
of golden afternoons
before your laughter
faded into cryptic silence
in an unforeseen interlude.

The Raven

The weight of his soul

dragged his feet

across the floor

burdening

his restless footsteps

with premonitions

dark and unholy

doomed to wander

evermore.

Inspiration and damnation

are two sides

of the same brush

upon which the poet

breaks her heart

to colour her canvas.

We have mastered the craft
of dancing upon eggshells
across broken bridges
we're too scared to burn.

They were but two ships
sailing into the melancholy night
parallel lines
on an unchartered course
destined to forever remain
under different skies.

Drifting thoughts
land at your doorstep
seeking refuge
in your memory
but knowing better
than to venture in
and make nostalgia
their home.

Liberate me

from the torment

into which my feet

sink deliriously

in their search

for the shade of your shadow

foolishly resigned

to hours of repentance

when your rapture fades

from my touch.

Her eyes were full

of faraway thoughts

fluttering away

on an autumn breeze

as the fading sun

stretches out

pale and wan

by the imprints of her feet.

Her only reprieve

was to fall asleep

and lose herself

in gentle dreams

where his savage touch

could not follow.

He observed her
with silent apathy
tucking his hands
behind his head
as she rained kisses
upon his brow
tumbling into love
upon his bed.

In the search
for what we have lost
we reduce ourselves
to a world
where we choke
on our own poison
and call it nostalgia.

Lint

She tried to hold on
her fingertips
grasping at air
when he let her go
discarding her affection
without a backward glance
like forgotten lint
in his back pocket.

He searches for her
in every woman
only to come back
to worship
at her feet.

Romeo

How bittersweet

when joy and sorrow mix,

star-crossed lovers

from the house of Montague and Capulet.

The exchange of vows

in the shroud of night,

amore under silver stars

tainted scarlet with familial strife.

A desperate plan

gone fatally awry

the angel of death

beckons to the sleeping bride.

Forever they shall remain

in sonnet and memory,

Juliet and her Romeo

under Verona's moonlit balcony.

These violent delights

have violent ends

consumed with fire

for precious slivers of heaven

comforted only by

hollow remembrance

and the forbidden perfume

of human skin.

Heathcliff

The love of the moors
bound their wild hearts
harnessed to a broken tree
tamed only by earthly separation
hark!
The lightning strikes
and Cathy beckons.

The text

Remedies for
instant gratification
lay at the tips
of her fingers
the catalyst
for emotional destruction
balanced precariously
on a blue send button.

Her expectations

remain crushed

under the weight

of his temporary affection,

hopelessly caught between

silver rubble

and bitter disappointment.

It was elementary

to see through him

for she knew

precisely where to look.

His memory

lingered bittersweet,

as fleeting

as a swan song

crying lullabies of

remorse and grief.

He built her castles
out of sand and cloud
a beauty to behold
but perilous to touch.

His brilliance faded from her eyes

and she could see

he was as ordinary

as the stones that lined the shore

a dime to a dozen

choking on their own seaweed.

'Twas not merely

the promise of today

he had stolen

but her hope for tomorrow,

though he searched for her in vain

her existence was

an exquisite pain

he was too young to follow.

We embark upon

the same treacherous path

guided by our broken feet

expecting a destination contrary

for what is the difference

between songs of hope

and hymns of insanity.

He emerges unscathed
while she unfolds
like a casualty
of the third world war.

Apathy crept

into her bones

dwelling

in their temporary home

until the call of dawn

flooded her skin anew

with hope.

She moved like a broken puppet

fragmented appendages

wrapped in flesh

held together

by frayed string

bound by good intentions.

Miss Havisham

All that she had hoped

glimmered beyond her reach

for the past brimmed

with faded luster

as the dream of love

lay dormant at her feet.

The lesson to learn, dear one

is that no two moments

are ever the same

for human hearts

know only how to

break, bleed

and change.

Appetite

Too much
was still too little
to fill the cavity
between her hollow ribs.

Tinted skies

dappled sunlight

and the caress

of the summer wind

are beautiful reminders

the world continues

to evolve and turn

with or without

your existence.

The human heart

is a labyrinth

of muscle and sentiment

where a single turn

can lead to

the heights of rapture

or the unforgiving depths

of mortal ruin.

Protagonist

He was a paradox
of hero and villain
weaving through
her poetry and prose
in effortless contradiction.

Disaster

She asked him why
he stood a little too close
locking her into place
with transfixed eyes so blue
as her heart withered
into decay,
he replied
she was a beautiful disaster
unfolding before him
compelled by curiosity
his heart was obliged to stay.

His mood shifted
with the phases of the moon
churning the waters
with waves of inconsistency
as she washed up
along the wretched shores
of his emotional purgatory.

Endless rivers

of silence

stretched between them

across his faded couch

with spaghetti stains

too fragile to cross

these perilous waters

were their tongues

whose words

had been left for dead

in past journeys

across his bed.

He shrouded her
in acidic silence
turning his sights
onto the greener pastures
of solitude.

He spends his days

in a grey fortress

a ruler blind

to the ruin of his kingdom

where everything he loves

shrivels to dust

under a thwarted Midas regime.

His memory

shall not be tyrannized

by the tongues

of those

who wish me well.

For the sake of tomorrow

we must say goodbye today.

Warrior

She wore her battles
like proud scars
that seared her skin
with tattoos of victory.

Naught a word was spoke
betwixt him and I
while the song of a sparrow
pierced the heavy silence
a lone witness
as the winter clouds
sorrowfully passed us by.

She merely requested
freedom from her thoughts
at a price her lungs
were too weary to pay
the debt lingered
as ash claimed her
while all shades of remembrance
leisurely faded away.

Calm thy expectations
as you gaze wistfully
towards the dawn
for people are
tricks of light
disguised as the sun.

Daisy

She was the dream
he could never realize
for Gatsby was a slave
to the whims of fantasy
obsessed with recreating a past
that collapsed to dust
at the edge of a green light
where his beloved lay
years ahead out of reach.

Wild

To tame one such as her
was sure to end in defeat
for how could he hope
to capture a turbulent heart
lost to the lure of sweet prose
and the wildness of the sea.

He tried to erase

the spectre

of your fingertips

from my skin

never knowing

your touch

trickled down

to the bone.

Pisces

Like a fish out of water
she was out of her element
trapped in a moment
where she thought she could hear
the whisper of the ocean
in his voice
and taste the salt
of the stormy sea
upon his skin.

Celebrate those
who have let you go
for they are the ones
who have set your spirit
free.

How tempting

it is to sink

beneath the murky depths

submerging oneself

wholly into the singing water

in the final dance

between life

and death.

Content with her discontent
she slipped into a waking coma
where life was a series of events
and she a distant voyeur
impervious to its joys
passive to its torments.

The sky was swollen with thunder
ominous clouds cautioned
to advance no further
before she soaked
cloth, skin and bone,
she was not one to heed warning
and laughed in the face of danger
dancing barefoot
in the eye of the storm.

Purple clouds bruise the sky

with the promise of rain

a redemption

she awaits with open palms

while adrenaline courses

through her veins.

We are all touched
by the gentle hand
of imperfection
seeking always
to capture a beauty
we already possess.

Sunlight filtered through her
in burnished shades of honey
that danced upon her skin
illuminating a captive heart
that beat in darkness within.

Lead me down the path
to the symphony of spring
where the brooks babble
and the birds sing
where sunflowers grow
in glorified abundance
revelling in the gentle sway
of Nature's budding romance.

In the eyes of Nature
we are true equals
each of us worthy
of a peaceful sunset
and deserving
of a new dawn.

Bound by bone

and blood

we are

all humans

brushed by a kiss

of stardust.

Summer Song

The amethyst sky spilled into blue
as twilight fell upon the hills
Nature's luminescent brew
heralded a warm summer spell.
casting over the carefree joys of youth.

Waves of sea cloud
broke in hues
of deep violet
and cobalt blue
as her eyes traced
the heart of the sky
and whispered wishes
upon the dying sun
for she was a child
born of moonlight
and superstition.

The sky cracked
with lightning bright
while the clouds wept
into the midsummer night,
all creatures trembled
in awe of the sublime
as their humbled heads
worshipped softly
at Nature's temple
in psalms of rhyme.

Her lips curved
and danced
on the edge of laughter
while the soft sunlight
reflected his mirth
upon the cool surface
of unbroken waters
whose ebb and flow
replenished the earth.

By the dying embers

of a June afternoon

the world continues to shift

on Fortune's axis

and tonight

we all play the Fool.

Children of the earth
sing songs of sunlight
and dance in meadows
of cornflowers
wearing garlands of daisies
their laughter burning bright
for endless hours
before plastic screens
whisk them all away.

God of War

The sky bled rain
and torn clouds shrouded the sun
the world turned on itself
in a relentless war
won by none.

Mad Men

Mad men dance to the tune of war
while the world waits
for their song to end.

We find ourselves
stumbling through lingering shadows
of all that is lost
caught between errors of judgement
and accidents of stars.

To be the son of Adam

and have the ambition

of a dragon

where our flawed nature

is inclined to breathe fire

only to exhale

air.

He lacked the curiousity
of human consciousness
to search beyond
dogma and scripture
content with the traditions
of old men and faulty literature.

We carry the burden

of premonition

where the

deaf and ignorant

deny consequence

and breed manipulation

consumed by

ego and arrogance

content to watch

the world burn

to feed their

sadistic satisfaction.

The Great Pretender

He was one
caught on the edge of night
in the mortal search
for his heart's delight
crafting melodies
of sublime creation
balanced precariously
betwixt the heavens
and hedonistic celebration.

The taste of the world

was bitter

against her chapped lips

stinging her

with spurned hope

and the tantalizing illusion

of promise.

Doors and passwords
are illusions of privacy
the notion we are safe
a childhood flight of fancy
for we are ensnared
in spider webs of
vigilantes and villains
in a world destined for decay.

They turned to the sea
to bring forth a man of worth
for the heavens had failed
sending them demons
parading in human disguise
wreaking havoc upon the earth.

Montmartre

Dusty sunlight
fell in patches
on the winding streets
of old Paris
creating rainbows
on pavements
that knew only grey.

Paris

The burden of time
ceased to press upon
her shoulders
for the city
felt like the sweet ache
of first love requited
and happiness like a dear friend
who drew her closer.

Florence

The bells sound in the distance
to rouse the city from her slumber
the chimes echo along the streets
where the children play
and the poets weep
as the world begins anew
glazed with wonder.

We are ships

blazing forth into the night

holding the sea for ransom

while we defy the constitution of stars

in the search for immorality

sailing upon treacherous courses

chartered by the arrogance of humanity.

Their words of caution

were lost like confetti

on the eve of the New Year

where her resolutions scattered

like crushed glass

on the floor.

Consequence

He views his reckless abandon
as a right for independence
searching for temporary freedom
in the arms of instant gratification
but rebellion is merely a romantic word
for the perils of self-destruction.

Time is a luxury
we can ill afford
and yet
we squander the hours
as though we possess
the ability to go back
and request a refund.

We seek our reflection
in broken mirrors
piecing together
the scattered fragments
of who we think we are.

Pilgrims

The stars were jewels

winking across the velvet night

as the humans below

contemplated secrets

hidden beyond the seventh sky,

their only map

was tried and tested faith

their key

was the lines of glory and sorrow

etched across each hopeful face.

Destination

They reached the end
of the horizon
and conquered
perils of the sea
with humble hearts
and weary feet.

Tradition

We rebel

against our very natures

to prove

we are different from our fathers

and their fathers before,

condemned

as straying children

in the struggle to create

our own natural discourse.

Welcome people
as they come,
embrace them
as they inevitably go,
for the natural trajectory
of friends and lovers
is to become strangers
once more.

How easily we fail to remember
that we are the architects
of our own happiness.

www.ingramcontent.com/pod-product-compliance
Lightning Source LLC
Chambersburg PA
CBHW032139040426
42449CB00005B/315